To

Ramsey Ella

Love ♡ xoxo

From

Grandma & Papa

Date

April 16, 2017

# Getting to Know Jesus for Little Ones

Brad and Kathy Bright
Based on the *Four Spiritual Laws* by Bill Bright
and the *4Keys 4Kids* by Bright Media Foundation®
Illustrations by Tracy Bishop

HARVEST HOUSE PUBLISHERS
EUGENE, OREGON

We dedicate this to Brad's mother, Vonette Bright, who in the busyness of reaching out to a lost and hurting world, never forgot about her own children and their need to know Jesus too.

Getting to Know Jesus for Little Ones

Text copyright © 2015 by Bright Media Foundation®
Artwork copyright © 2015 by Tracy Bishop

Published by Harvest House Publishers
Eugene, Oregon 97402
www.harvesthousepublishers.com

ISBN 978-0-7369-5401-3

Design and production by Mary pat Pino, Mary pat Design, Westport, CT

**Printed in China.**

14 15 16 17 18 19 20 21 22 / DS / 10 9 8 7 6 5 4 3 2 1

# A note just for you…

Brad was three and a half years old when, in the middle of a pillow fight, his brother announced, "Me, Mommy, and Daddy are going to heaven, but you're not!" Devastated, Brad ran to tattle on his brother. His mom took him on her knee and asked, "Would you like to know for sure that you will go to heaven?" Brad had often heard the story of Jesus, but now he understood for the first time that he needed to personally ask Jesus to be his Savior.

Kathy was the first in her family to accept Christ. She was eight when, during an occasional visit to Sunday school, she heard the message of Jesus for the first time. That night, alone in her bed, she asked Jesus to forgive her sins, come into her heart, and be with her forever.

Our job is to teach the children we love who God really is and why they need a Savior. When they express a desire to trust in Christ we can experience the joy of introducing them to Jesus and then helping them grow in that relationship.

One of our greatest privileges was showing our children, Keller and Noël, how to begin a relationship with God. We pray that as you read this book to your precious little ones, they too will place their trust in Jesus. A life built on Him will give them a rock solid foundation!

We have wrapped the Gospel message (based on the *4Keys 4Kids* and *The Four Spiritual Laws*) in a fanciful story to help engage the hearts and minds of the children you love. If you have any questions or need help with next steps, please visit us online at: dg4kids.com.

– Brad and Kathy

3

Tommy and Keesha
And Marco and Su
Were looking for God,
But they needed a clue.

They wanted to know Him,
The Creator of all,
And be His close friend
Even though they were small.

Someone who's older and wiser than they
Said that four keys would show them the way.
Finding **Key One** is where they must start.
Look for the key that's shaped like a heart.

# KEY ONE
## God loves you.

Because God is love,
He wants you to know
He loves you from the top of your head
To the tippy-tip-tip of each toe.

God loves to watch you giggle.
He's happy when you're kind.
He's sad when you're mean to others,
But even then you'll find
His love for you stays the same.
It's the first amazing key.
God loves you. He loves me.
God loves everyone you see!

*For God loved the world so much that
He gave His one and only Son [Jesus],
so that everyone who believes in Him
will not perish but have eternal life.*
John 3:16

They all wanted to hold it,
But Tommy grabbed it first.
"I'll keep it safe," he told them,
"In the pocket of my shirt."

"Oh, no, you don't!" the others cried.
And so the fight began.
Each tried hard to take it
From the grip of Tommy's hand.

The special key flew from his grasp
And popped up in the air.
A mighty wind picked it up
And took it far from there.

It blew across a canyon,
So dark and oh so wide.
How could they ever get it
So far on the other side?

Keesha stood next to Tommy.
Marco stood next to Su.
They hung their heads and saw it—
The canyon was **Key Two!**

# KEY TWO
## Sin keeps us from God.

Sin is when we're mean,
When we lie or cheat or fight.
It's like saying "NO!" to God
And doing wrong, not right.

God is clean—like fresh, clear water.
He's always good and true.
There's nothing bad or wrong with Him.
Not so for me and you!

Our sin keeps us away from God.
It's the sad and second key.
Turn the page and you will see
Hope is in **Key Three!**

*For everyone has sinned;
we all fall short of God's
glorious standard.*
Romans 3:23

Marco's mom brought out a snack
And told them not to worry.
"Take a seat and eat your treat,
And I'll tell you a true story."

14

"Once upon a time," she said,
"God sent His only Son
To show how much He loves us,
Each and every one."

"Jesus Christ is perfect.
He's always good and true.
That's why He could pay sin's price.
He paid it for me and you."

"Did it cost Him lots of money?"
Su wanted to know.
"And all His toys?" cried Marco.
"What about His home?"

"He paid the price with His life,"
She told them quietly.
"He made the way to God's great love,
So that's why He's **Key Three!**"

The friends looked to the canyon,
And there before their eyes,
A blood-red key stretched like a bridge,
Reaching side to side.

# KEY THREE
## Jesus is the only way!

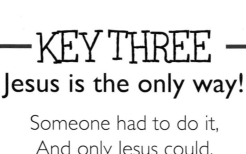

Someone had to do it,
And only Jesus could.
No one else was perfect,
So Jesus said He would!

Dying on the cross, He paid
For all the sins we've done.
Then He came alive again—
God's one and only Son!

Jesus is the only way.
He's the wonderful **Key Three**.
But before we can know God's love,
There's one more key we'll need.

*But God showed His great love for us
by sending Christ [Jesus] to die for
us while we were still sinners.*

Romans 5:8

*Jesus told him, "I am the way, the truth,
and the life. No one can come to
the Father except through Me."*

John 14:6

The friends all ran to see it,
But the way across was blocked.
A door filled the pathway.
It was big and heavy and locked.

"Oh, no!" they cried.
Then Keesha spied
Four boxes in a row
Sitting by the doorway—

And tied with yellow bows.
"Let's open them!" they shouted,
And that's just what they did.
They tore the paper and pulled the bows,
Then lifted up the lids.

"It's **Key Four!**" They laughed out loud,
Each holding a yellow key.
Marco's mom smiled and said,
"There's something God wants you to see."

# KEY FOUR
## You must say "yes" to Jesus!

Jesus is God's gift to you.
He wants to be your friend,
But if the gift is to be yours,
Accept His payment for your sins.

Say "yes" that you are sorry
For all the sins you've done
And "yes" you trust Him to forgive
Each and every one.

Say "no" to all that's sinful.
Ask His help and you will find
He'll give the strength you will need
Each and every time!

*But to all who believed Him and accepted Him, He gave the right to become children of God.*
John 1:12

Tommy and Keesha
And Marco and Su
Found all four keys,
And they knew what to do.

They got on their knees
And bowed their heads.
They talked to God,
And this is what they said…

27

# PRAYER

"Yes, Lord Jesus, I need You.
Yes, I want to be Your friend.
Thank You for dying on the cross
And paying for my sins.

"Yes, I open up the door of my heart.
Please be my friend and King.
Help me to obey You
And trust You with everything.

"Yes, I want to know You better
Each and every day.
Yes, I want to love You more.
Please help me listen and obey."

[Jesus promises,]
*"Look! I stand at the door and
knock. If you hear My
voice and open the door,
I will come in…"*
Revelation 3:20

The friends all jumped for joy
When the door swung open wide.
The adventure was just beginning
As they crossed the great divide.

*"...I will never fail you.*
*I will never abandon you."*
Hebrews 13:5

What about you? Would you like to get to know God and His great love for you? If you do, you can talk with God right now like the friends did. If you mean what you say, you can be sure Jesus will forgive your sins and be with you wherever you go —now and forever!

Today I said "yes" to Jesus!
I asked Him to forgive my sins
and become my King.
I know God loves me, and
He will always be my best friend.

Name:

_____

Date:

_____